DEDICATION

———————

To the one aspiring to live a victorious and fulfilled

life...add the Lord Jesus Christ to the

roster of your heart. He is the ULTIMATE!

"Surely he hath borne our griefs, and carried

our sorrows...and with his stripes

we are healed."

Isaiah 53:4-5

CONTENTS

———————

in the LORD JESUS!!

As you read the book, I will share with you some of my personal experiences as a youth and young adult and invite your own reflections during a segment entitled, " 🏈 **On the Field!**".

I welcome you to be real about your own life experiences in the " ✖ **Pick Up that Blitz!**" segment. These are designed for you to identify challenging areas in your life that blitz you head on; causing you to cry out to the Lord to help you pick up that blitz!

ACKNOWLEDGMENTS

I want to thank the Lord for allowing me the opportunity to serve in the marketplace and to those who encouraged me during my youth and young adult years...God Bless You!!

in the LORD JESUS!!

1- Two Opposing Forces

P erhaps no other sport can electrify a crowd like the game of football. Football is a sport played by two opposing teams of eleven players on a rectangular field with goalposts at each end. The offense, the team with possession of the oval-shaped football, attempts to advance down the field through space and time created by the offensive line; by running with the ball or passing it, while the defense, the team without possession of the ball, aims to stop the offense's advance and take control of the ball for themselves.

The offense must advance at least ten yards in four downs or plays. If they fail, they turn over the football to the defense, but if they succeed, they are given a new set of four downs to continue the drive. Points are scored primarily by advancing the ball into the opposing team's end zone for a touchdown or kicking the ball through the opponent's goalposts for a field goal. The team with the most points at the end of a game wins.

If you think about it, life is very similar to football. Just as the game cannot start until the ball is in position, your physical life could not start until you were born. Now once the ball is snapped from the hands of the Center, the defense is released to test the determination and strategy of the offense.

When you were born, your offense stepped onto the field. God had an offensive strategy for your life, to be victorious! **John 3:16** says, *"For God so loved the world, that he gave his only begotten Son, that whosoever believeth in him should not perish, but have everlasting life."* God's strategy for your life includes accepting his son Jesus Christ as your Lord and Savior. However, the defensive minded devil wants to use his team to oppose that strategy at the line of scrimmage. He desires to stop the advancement of God's purpose for your life and take control of it himself, leading to your ultimate defeat.

Now let's set the stage here. The devil (serpent) is the evil influence that brought the option of sin into the world through temptation (Genesis 3:1-6). Sin is disobedience to God. Temptation is encouragement to do sin. Sin has many varieties known as behaviors. These behaviors make up the devil's team. Sinful (unrighteous) behavior begins with a thought or imagination that encourages the individual to behave in a manner that is unacceptable to God. Unrighteous simply means, it ain't right!!

When the individual does not take a stand against the thought or imagination and yields to it continually, it can push the individual into an unrighteous lifestyle. Unrighteous living with no action to change for the better is called iniquity. Iniquity will push you backwards, straight into the locker room of Hell. Jesus said in **Matthew 13:41**, *"The Son...shall gather out of his kingdom all...them which do iniquity; and...cast them into a furnace of fire..."* That furnace of fire is the locker room of Hell. Now, understand that Jesus did not come to condemn. To condemn means to make unfit for use. He came to alert us of sinful behaviors (Mark 7:21-23) that cause condemnation and to instruct us to turn away from such living. Turning away is known as repentance.

According to **Matthew 4:17**, *"Jesus began to preach,*

and to say, Repent...” Now, when Jesus gives the 411 and the individual still chooses to live in and love sin rather than God, the individual, through the power of choice, begins the condemnation process. Jesus said in **John 3:19**, *“And this is the condemnation, that light is come... the world...loved darkness rather than light...”* Jesus Christ is the light. Sin is darkness. So, in Matthew 13:41, Jesus carries out the consequence of the individual's choice to live a life devoted to sin (darkness) rather than Christ (light).

Even if you are already a Christian, do not let the devil fool you by thinking you can do whatever and not be condemned. **Romans 8:1** says, *“There is therefore now no condemnation to them which are in Christ Jesus, **who walk not after the flesh**, but after the Spirit.”* This means those who strive each day to live a godly life. However, if you choose to consistently walk in sin as a Christian, check out

Matthew 7: 22-23, *“Many will say to me...Lord, Lord, have we not prophesied in thy name? and in thy name have cast out devils? and in thy name done many wonderful works?*

And then will I profess unto them, I never knew you: depart from me, ye that work iniquity." My brothers and sisters in Christ, do not be cast away.

The devil's goal is to prevent you from entering the ultimate endzone of heaven and keep you ultimately bound in the locker room of Hell. But stand your ground and compete! There is a fierce gridiron battle going down, and the line of scrimmage is waiting for you. It's your offense vs. the devil's defense.

in the LORD JESUS!!

2- Your Offense

Your offensive strategy starts with a strong offensive line. As I said earlier, in football, the offensive line can push the defense back, create space for the running game, and create time for the passing game. In your life, you need an offensive line that can push back on the pressures of life and create doors of opportunities and time for you to advance forward! Let's look at a sample offensive line:

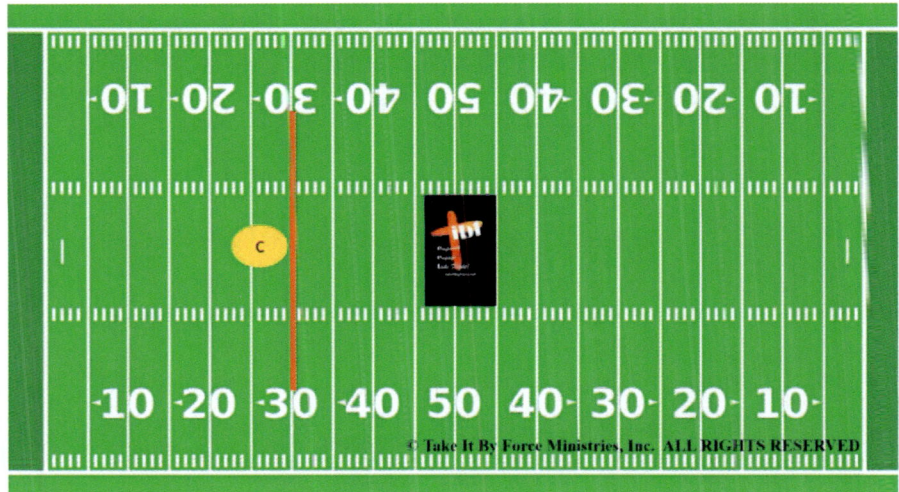

Graphic (1)

At the red line of scrimmage, your first offensive lineman in graphic (1) is the **(C) - Center**. This player holds the football before each play begins on the field. Who holds your life? Don't allow your life to fall into the wrong hands by associating with and taking bad advice from the wrong crowd. Allow **Jesus** to be the *center* of your joy!

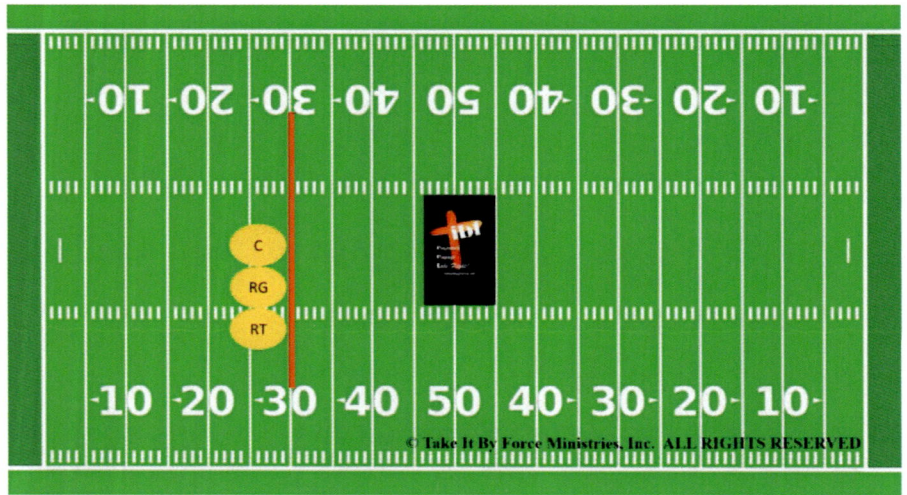

Graphic (2)

Next up, we have in graphic (2) the **(RG)- Right Guard** and **(RT)- Right Tackle.** These players pick up the defensive pressure coming from the right side of the line. Learn how to *guard* your heart against the darkness of this world by allowing Jesus to come in. Jesus says in **Revelation 3:20**, *"Behold, I stand at the door, and knock: if any...hear my voice, and open the door, I will come in to him, and will sup with him, and he with me."* The Lord desires to come into the heart of the individual for a true relationship, a relationship that offers godly knowledge and wisdom. Knowledge is simply information. Wisdom is the best way to utilize information.

Tackle obstacles in life with a Christ like mindset, knowing that Jesus has already given you the victory. Jesus told his disciples in **John 16:33**, *"In the world ye shall have tribulation: but be of good cheer; I have overcome the world."* He wanted them to know that pressure is coming, but they can get through it! On the field called life, the defense is coming, but your offense has got to withstand!

On the Field! - I remember when I was in high school, and I allowed my life to fall into the hands of the wrong center. She was a very attractive young lady, and I found myself doing things that were no longer pleasing to God. She and I were pleased naturally, walking in iniquity but the relationship was a spiritual disaster. Jesus was no longer my center, she was! I felt like my life was being fumbled away. That's what happens when you allow your life to fall into the wrong hands. It's a fumble! Thankfully, I dropped her, picked up my relationship with Jesus and moved on.

On the Field! – Can you recall a time when your life had fallen into the wrong hands? It was one fumble after another. Were you able to get back on track? Why or Why not?

_____

_____

_____

_____

_____

_____

_____

_____

_____

_____

_____

_____

_____

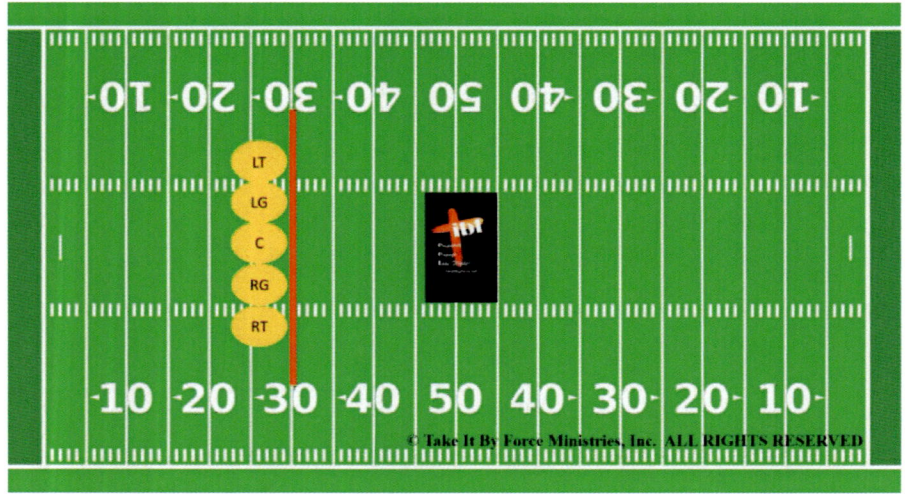

Graphic (3)

The above graphic includes the **(LG)– Left Guard** and **(LT)- Left Tackle** positions. Again, the idea is to have adequate protection **across** the line. In times like these you need *a cross* to turn to. That cross is Jesus.

Now that you have your offensive line in place, it's time to move down the field.

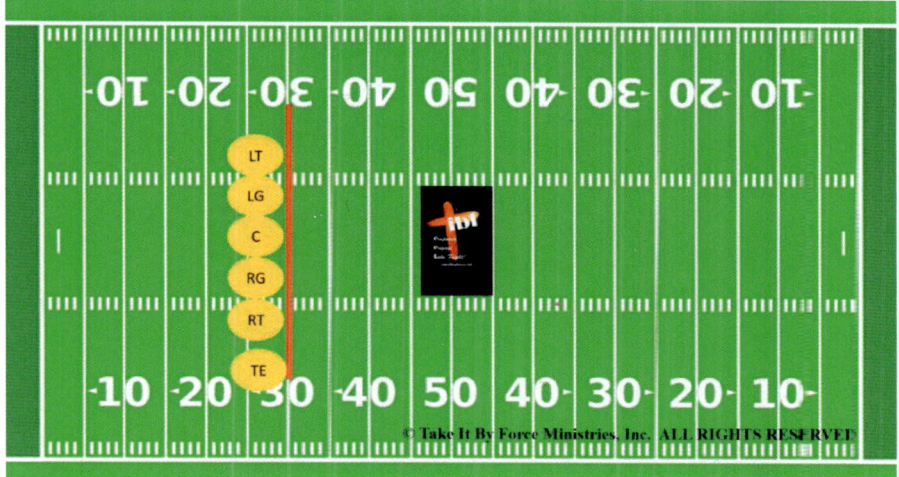

Graphic (4)

The **(TE)-Tight End** position in graphic (4) serves a couple of roles. This position can serve as an extra blocker for the offensive line or catch the ball as a receiver. **Isaiah 40:31** declares, *"But they that wait upon the Lord shall renew their strength; they shall mount up with wings as eagles..."* Ah yes, wings as eagles, take flight, that's the air attack, the passing game, your wide receiver core! The receivers can get you down the field quick, fast and in a hurry! And just like the wind, they can move in any direction.

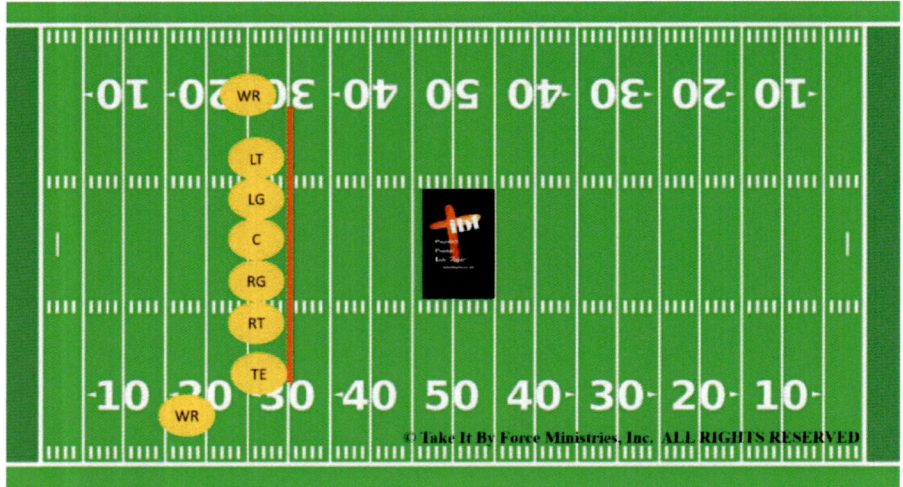

Graphic (5)

There are two **(WR)-Wide Receivers** in graphic (5), along with the TE. Nobody can move you like the Lord. He can help you get things done when no one else can. But you must have a relationship with him and learn how to wait on (serve) him. Serve him not because of what he can do for you, but simply because of who he is. He is the ultimate!

The next major player on your offense is the **(QB)-Quarterback**. The QB in graphic (6) is positioned behind the center and initiates the offensive play upon verbal command.

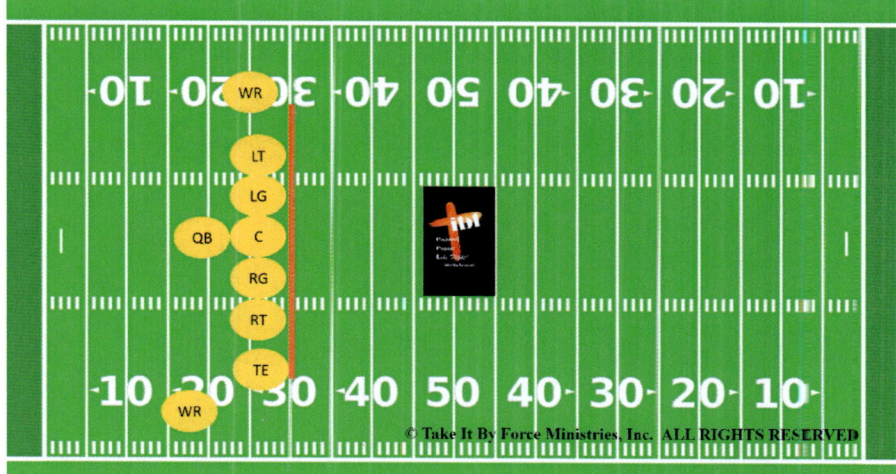

Graphic (6)

The QB must have the mental capacity to recognize the defensive scheme in front and determine if the initial play called in is suitable enough to gain yardage or if there is a need to change the play (audible). The QB must be comfortable enough with the team playbook to know what audible action to take. It's important to know when your life is headed down the wrong road and have a sense of urgency to change directions. Your life is too valuable to waste it following behind the wrong crowd or engaging in sinful behavior that leads to destruction. Be smart with the choices you make like a QB must be smart with the football!

Positioned behind the QB in graphic (7) is the **(FB)-Fullback**.

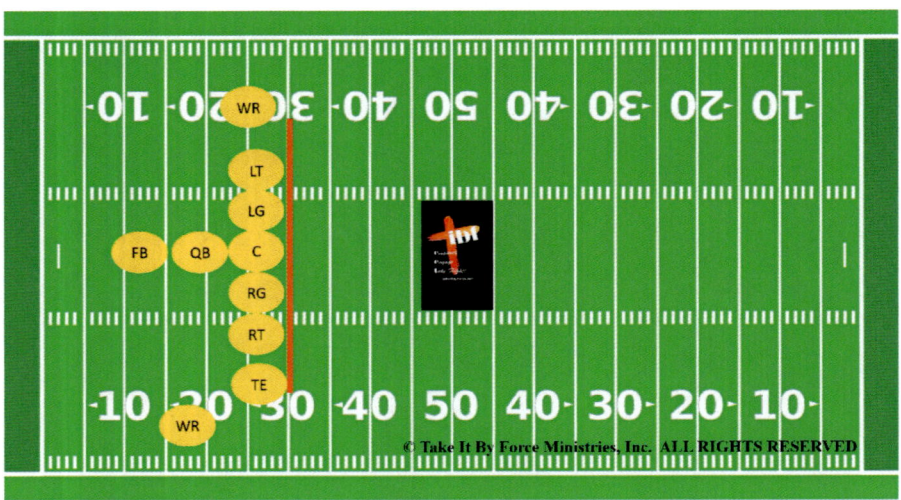

Graphic (7)

Depending on the offensive play, the fullback can serve as an extra blocker or open the run game, which makes the offense more difficult to defend against. An offense that runs and throws the football can be very successful. Know when it's time to run in life. **Isaiah 40:31** further declares, *"..they shall run.."* Having a relationship with the Lord gives you the option to run from tempting people, mindsets, and situations. Now, whether you choose the option, is on you!

Next up is the **(HB)- Halfback**. From behind the FB in graphic (8), the HB typically runs the football.

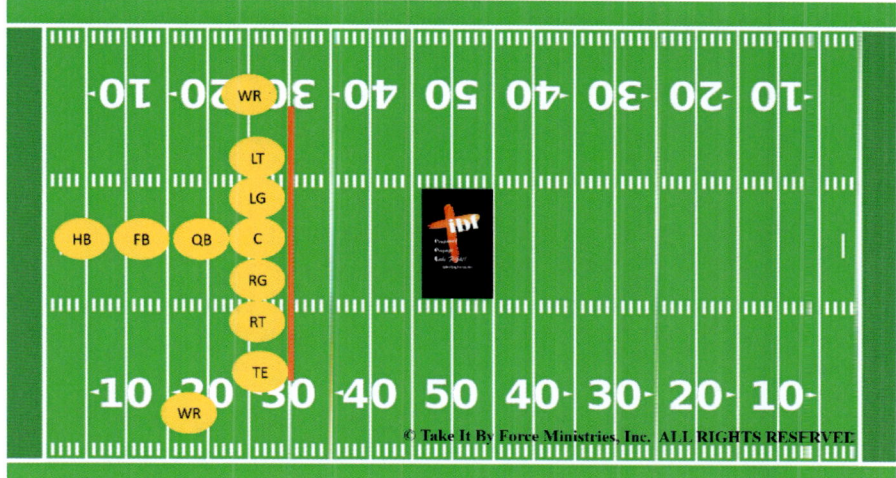

Graphic (8)

When the offensive lineman creates a door of opportunity, the running back secures the handoff from the QB and sprints through it like a jet! The Lord knows how to securely get your life from one point to the other. Put it in his hands.

On the Field! – I received my handoff of opportunity and ran with it like a HB! I remember when I got ready to apply to college. I had a lot of advice regarding where to go. Since I was ten years old, I had the desire to go to North Carolina State University. Many discouraged me from applying, but I was not going to let that hinder me. I knew that my standardized test scores were low, and my GPA was below the minimum requirement. Nevertheless, God had a strategy for my life. When I *opened* my acceptance letter that summer of 1991, I took off *running* around the house, ran straight up highway 64 west, through New Bern Ave., down Hillsborough St, right to Metcalf Dormitory and into the graduation *endzone* in May 1995 with my business degree in hand! And I'm still running! God has been GOOD to me! It's a FIRST DOWN in the Lord Jesus!

On the Field! — Have you ever had a good opportunity open for you? Talk about it.

_____

_____

_____

_____

_____

_____

_____

_____

in the LORD JESUS!!

3- Put Your Gear On

Now that your offense is in tack; you cannot hit the field without proper equipment. Let's use graphic (9) below and scripture from **Ephesians 6:13-17** to gear up!

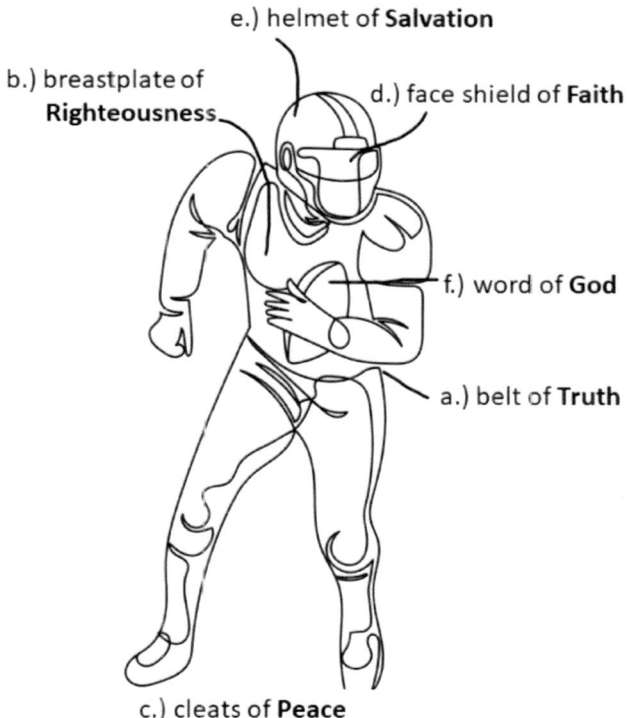

Graphic (9)

The scripture says, *"13 Wherefore take unto you the whole armour of God, that ye may be able to withstand in the evil day, and having done all, to stand.*

14 Stand therefore...with truth, and having on the breastplate of righteousness;

15 And your feet...with...the gospel of peace;

16 Above all, taking the shield of faith, wherewith ye shall be able....

17 And take the helmet of salvation...which is the word of God"

To get things going, put on:

    a.) belt of **Truth** (v.14) - Take the right stance. When confronted with tempting and dishonest opportunities, allow honesty to fasten you in as you maneuver your way through life. Be sincere in your conversations and seek to learn the truth in God's word.

    b.) breastplate of **Righteousness** (v.14) - Have a heart that is willing to learn right from wrong and dedicate yourself to doing right, even when it brings unpopularity.

c.) cleats of **Peace** (v.15) - Use Christ as an example to be a solution when confronted with problems in the home, school, church, or community in general. Wherever you go, bring peace in the form of value (added ideas and a concern for others) with you, not chaos and iniquity!

d.) face shield of **Faith** (v.16) - Trust in the Lord even when things in life look crazy! **Hebrews 11:6** says, *"... without faith it is impossible to please him: for he that cometh to God must believe that he is, and that he is a rewarder of them that diligently seek him."*

e.) helmet of **Salvation** (v.17) - Know what God's plan of salvation is: **John 3:16**, which says, *"For God so loved the world, that he gave his only begotten Son, that whosoever believeth in him should not perish, but have everlasting life."* Strap on a relationship with Christ. That relationship requires your time and effort and teaches you how to identify what is godly (good) and ungodly (bad). Salvation serves as a reminder that your life matters, and God cares about you, even when you may not care about yourself. That reminder was key for me when I thought about committing suicide in college.

On the Field! – I put on my helmet of salvation when I was 13. I accepted Jesus as my savior at that time, which proved to be the most important decision of my life. Did it mean I was perfect? No. But it taught me how to look, listen, learn from my environment and filter out negative things. A few years later, my mother gave me a Bible for Christmas. It was the perfect complement to my helmet.

f.) word of **God** (v.17) - Just like the player in graphic (9) is holding the football, hold God's word close to your heart. Jesus said in **Matthew 22:37**, *"Thou shalt love the Lord thy God with all thy heart..."* The word of God can benefit your heart by identifying thoughts and intentions in there that are not right.

The football gives the player a reason to be on the field, get in the game, be competitive, and strive for victory! Without the ball, there is no game! God's word gives you a reason to wake up every morning, get out of bed, be productive, and walk in victory! **Genesis 2:27** says, *"Be fruitful.."* which means, make godly choices in life and contribute something positive to society. It does not mean to have a bunch of babies outside of marriage.

On the Field! —Always remember that prayer is important also. **Ephesians 6:18** says, *"Praying always...and watching..."* Prayer is simply communication with God. You can pray at any place and time. If you don't know where to start, try this: *Lord, I thank you for waking me up today and providing me with what I need. Forgive me of any wrongdoing and teach me how to forgive others and walk in your ways. Protect us all. In Jesus name, Amen.*

There are some wonderful prayer scriptures in the Bible. Two of my favorites are: **Matthew 6:9-13** and **Psalm 23**. Check them out!

in the LORD JESUS!!

4 - The Devil's Defense

The Apostle Paul was a great literary contributor to the Bible. As an Apostle, his role was to establish churches and follow up with them periodically (to ensure spiritual growth). He did not want people to live in ignorance and deception. Ignorance is when you do not know. Deception is being led in the wrong direction.

In a letter he wrote to a church in the geographical region of Corinth, Paul clears the air by pointing out various unrighteous behaviors that serve on the devil's team as defensive barriers between God and the people.

The behaviors are designed to push the individual further and further away from a relationship with God. Of course, the devil does not want you to have anything to do with God! **1Peter 5:8** says... *"your adversary the devil, as a roaring lion, walketh about, seeking whom he may devour."*

The devil is out to defeat you, and he utilizes these behaviors to do so. In **1Corinthians 6: 9** Paul says, *"Know ye not that the unrighteous shall not inherit the kingdom of God?"* Here we see where Paul challenges the knowledge level of the people. He lets them know that unrighteous behavior will keep them OUT of relationship with God. Next, he says, *"Be not deceived."* He did not want people to think that unrighteous behavior is okay! Be careful of deceptive people, those who tell you there is nothing wrong with doing unrighteous things.

We live in a time when immoral behavior is the norm. Immoral simply means *it ain't right*!! My goal is to describe the ten behaviors Paul mentions, so you will:

1.) Know what unrighteous behavior is, 2.) If engaged in the behavior, make the right decision to stop it and 3.) Encourage someone else who may be engaged in the behavior to stop as well.

Let's look at the devil's defensive lineup in graphic (10).

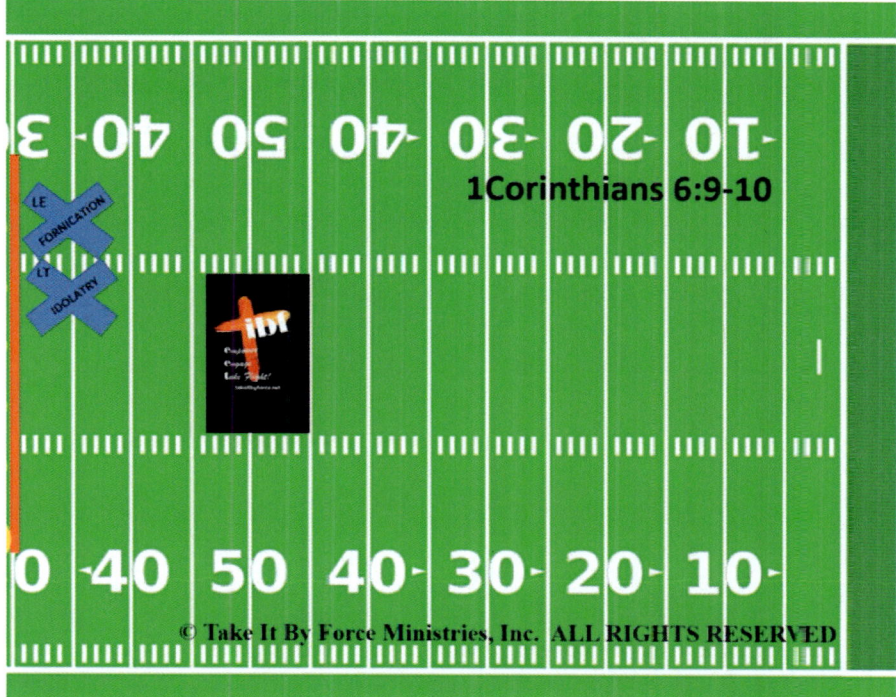

1Corinthians 6:9-10

Graphic (10)

In verse 9, Paul introduces the roster with the two most popular defensive linemen on the team:

The **(LE)-Left End** of **fornication** - Fornication is sex between an unmarried male and unmarried female. Sex is supposed to be between a husband and wife. According to **Genesis 4:1**, *"And Adam knew Eve his wife; and she conceived.."* In other words, Adam and Eve had sex, and she got pregnant. That is the proper order.

However, fornication tends to be high among the youth and young adult population in the US. As a result, statistics show that young people aged 15-24 years acquire half of all new sexually transmitted diseases (STD's) in the U.S., and one in four sexually active adolescents has an STD. Compared with older adults, sexually active adolescents aged 15-19 years and young adults aged 20-24 years are at higher risk of acquiring STD's.

I think three factors may contribute to this behavior: generational, environmental and personal choice. Some families may have a history of fornicating activity. Therefore, it can become an acceptable norm.

If the youth live in a single parent environment, the challenge for the single parent is to set a godly example. If the single father brings home a different woman every other night (or a woman whom he is not married to) and commits fornication in that environment, the youth may think that is acceptable behavior and model themselves after that lifestyle.

This means they are not being taught that fornication is wrong. The same could be said of a single mother with a man. Paul says in **1 Corinthians 6:18**, "Flee fornication."

My desire is that God would raise up a generation of youth who love him so much that they are not afraid to call out unrighteousness behavior, no matter where it is, even if it's in the home!

Conflict can occur in the home where righteousness and unrighteousness abide. But stand for righteousness anyway. Jesus said in **Matthew 10:35**, *"For I am come to set a man at variance against his father, and the daughter against her mother..."* Now what that means is this:

> Variance is disagreement between two occupants of the same house. Jesus comes with the word of God to teach both young and old about godly living. Some will grab the word; some will drop it. Those who grab it will stand up for what is right. Those who drop it will fall for what is wrong.

So, regarding the fornication example, if the son grabs the word of God and confronts, which is a BOLD move for righteousness, the father who drops the word, the two disagree. Likewise, if the daughter grabs the word and confronts the mother who drops it, the two also disagree. Somewhere in the disagreement, you hope the one in error will have a change of heart and do right. That's called repentance. Pray for that parent!

Now it could be where the parent grabs the word, and the youth drops it. In this case, there is disagreement, but the youth doesn't care and commits fornication anyway. That's called personal choice. Pray for that youth!

Formication and its teammates get their training from social media, music, TV, books, and magazines, which is full of crazy content. Even in a home where a godly example is established, the individual can be exposed to those aspects of society every day outside the home. The challenge goes like this:

1. Exposure to crazy social media, music, TV, books, and magazines

2. An unmarried individual wants to portray what the exposure suggests.

3. Connects with another unmarried individual who has the same idea

4. Fornication is committed and just pushed each individual back 15 yards.

5. If there is a weak offensive line (unwillingness to stop the behavior), fornication keeps on pushing each individual backward.

I know it's so because that's what happened to me back in chapter 2, when I was in high school.

Next up is the **(LT)- Left Tackle** of **idolatry** - Three words are in this one word: I, do, try. Idolatry is the worship of *I do try!* I do try this. I do try that. I do try everything and everybody else BUT God. He has no room in the chambers of your heart. The Lord says in **Exodus 20:3**, *"Thou shalt have no other gods before me."* An individual can fall in love with various gods: money, career, cars, houses, wardrobe, video game platforms, social media, job, and degrees; all while leaving out the most important one, God.

Matthew 6:33 says, *"But seek ye first the kingdom of God, and his righteousness; and... things shall be added unto you."* Seek to have a relationship with God first. Then, allow him to gradually add those things to you that will complement that relationship and not take away from it.

On the Field! – I remember when I first graduated from college. I had to have the coolest ride. It was a 1995 Toyota Corolla. It was a nice vehicle with all the accessories. But as time passed, I found myself always trading vehicles in for another one. Cars had become an idol. When I got married, my wife challenged me on those decisions. As my family grew, I changed my thinking and learned how to maintain the vehicles we had.

On the Field! – Is there an area in your life that has become an idol? How did it get to that point? What can you do to put the Lord back where he belongs?

Look at the **(RT)- Right Tackle** of **adultery** in graphic (11).

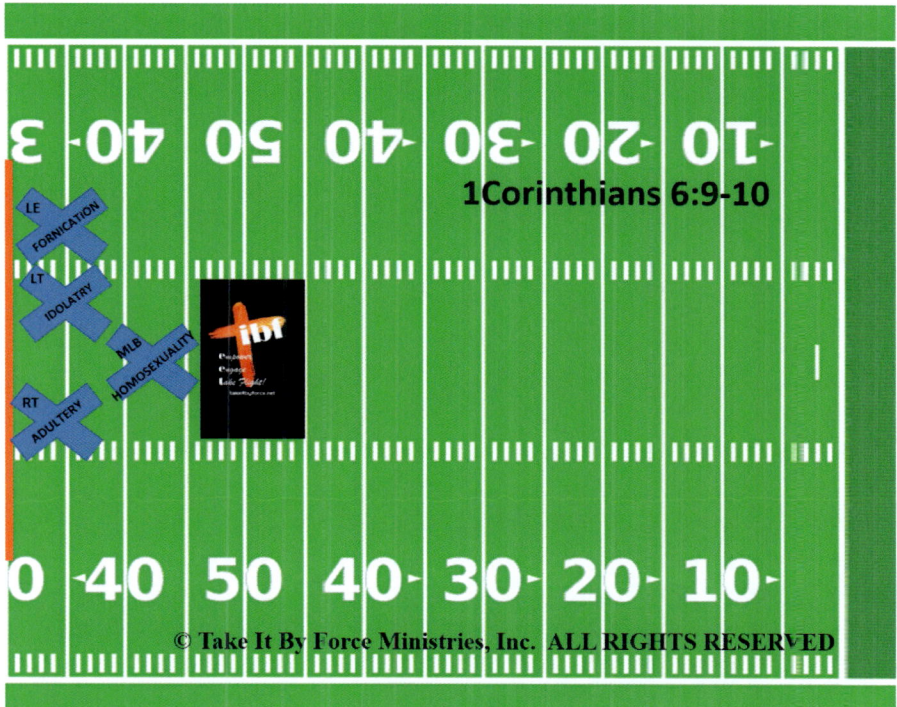

Graphic (11)

Adultery is designed specifically to attack marriage. Marriage is a relationship between one man (husband) and one woman (wife). **Genesis 2:24** clarifies this, *"Therefore shall a man leave his father and his mother and shall cleave unto his wife: and they shall be one..."* That is true marriage. Now, the physical act of sex is designed for a husband and his wife. According to **Genesis 4:1**, *"And Adam knew Eve his wife;*

and she conceived.." That means Adam had sex with his wife and she got pregnant. That is the proper order.

Now when either the husband or the wife decides to have a marital type of relationship with another individual while still being married, that is adultery. The Lord says in Exodus 20:14, *"Thou shalt not commit adultery."*

Next, we have the **(MLB)- Middle Linebacker** of **homosexuality**. Homosexuality is associated with the male tendency to direct sexual desire toward another male. **Leviticus 18:22** says, *"Thou shalt not lie with mankind, as with womankind: it is abomination."* Abomination is evil behavior. This type of lifestyle among females is called lesbianism. **Romans 1:26** mentions this unclean behavioral tendency, *"for even their women did change the natural use into that which is against nature..."*

The MLB is in a unique position on the field. Notice how it is situated further back than its teammates. That distance provides an opportunity for a BLITZ! A blitz is an intense overpowering rush of force towards the line of scrimmage, aimed at the QB and the ball! The middle linebacker of homosexuality has really blitzed its way into the lives of our youth, especially at the middle school level, where identity really begins to take form. When I was a volunteer at a local middle school, it saddened me to see so many youth of the same gender walking the halls holding hands.

Pick Up that Blitz! – The best way to pick up a blitz is to have a strong offensive lineman mentality where you stand firm like a tree and refuse to be dominated.

Psalms 1: 1-3 declares, *"Blessed is the man that walketh not in the counsel of the ungodly… his delight is in the law of the Lord…day and night..and he shall be like a tree planted by the rivers of water…and whatsoever he doeth shall prosper."*

You must be dedicated to your stance in the Lord with a desire to live right and cast aside evil imaginations, crazy thoughts and bad advice that comes at you. As a middle school youth I was confronted with homosexuality, but I stood my ground and pushed it out of my way. The Lord is your better option! Your delight must be in him. When it's not in him, the blitz will run you over; like fornication did to me. But when I got tired of being run over by fornication, I exercised my better option, got up from the turf, and pressed my way forward! The key is that you don't surrender your life to the devil's defense. Don't surrender your life to sin. God is telling you to GET UP!..and advance to the next down!!

Hurt, embarrassed, depressed or even suicidal...I've been there and know exactly what it feels like. But you can GET UP, execute the next play and move those chains! FIRST DOWN in the Lord Jesus! The resurrection of Christ is the Christian's play audible to get up from being run over by the devil's defense! Christ got up on the third down...the third day, with all power in his hands. Right where you are, lift both hands and say, "Lord help me to get up on this third down!" You may be at third and inches; push your way through. It may be third and long; exercise your faith and run a wheel route and go for the victory! Get Up! Get Up! Get Up! Clap your hands and give God a PRAISE!!

Football is a contact sport! As a Christian, you will not be perfect, and you will be knocked down. But get back up and keep pressing towards the endzone! Superbowl champions rarely go undefeated in a season but manage to rise to the occasion when it matters most! They have a heart for victory; you must have a heart for God!

Pick Up that Blitz! – Is there any area in your life that is constantly being blitzed? What can you do to help withstand the challenge?

_____

_____

_____

_____

_____

_____

_____

_____

Up next in graphic (12) is the **(RE)- Right End** of **self-abuse** and the **(LOLB)-Left Outer Linebacker** of **theft**.

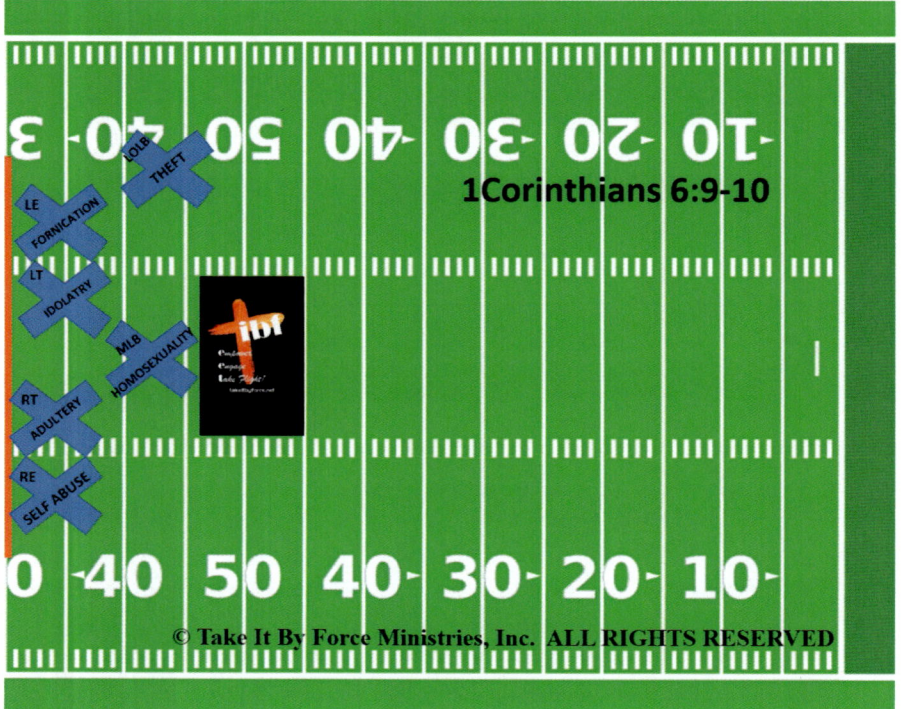

Graphic (12)

Self-abuse can take the form of drugs, alcohol, and smoking. Other forms of abuse that God does not like, which are common in society include:

1.) prostitution – This could hang out with fornication at the gym, (**Ezekiel 16:15**) Your life means more than allowing yourself to be physically and mentally misused by others. Ask the Lord to help you find that meaning!

2.) pornography (**Ezekiel 23:13-17**) - An evil influence in society, that brings corruption and shame. Self-worth should mean more than easy money and a cheap thrill. Come out of it! Turn it off!

3.) masturbation (**Genesis 38:9-10**) - A physical wasting away of time and energy. Get your hands out of your pants, wash them, and stop allowing your godly potential to fall to the ground. Replace your idle time with meaningful goal setting and a real blueprint to achieve them.

4.) transgender movement (**Deuteronomy 22:5**) - If God created you as a boy, grow up to become a man. If God created you as a girl, grow up to become a woman. Stand firm and push back on this self-abusive mindset that incorporates modern day medicines and procedures to reverse that which God has established.

5.) abortion (**Exodus 20:13**, **Matthew 18:5**) - You had no control over how you got here, but when given a little space and time, you learn what you can do now that you are here.

In 1Corinthians 6:10, Paul mentions theft. Stealing anything is not a healthy way of living. If you switch tags in the store just to get a cheaper price, that is a form of theft. Honesty is the best policy. **Exodus 20:15** clearly states, *"Thou shalt not steal."*

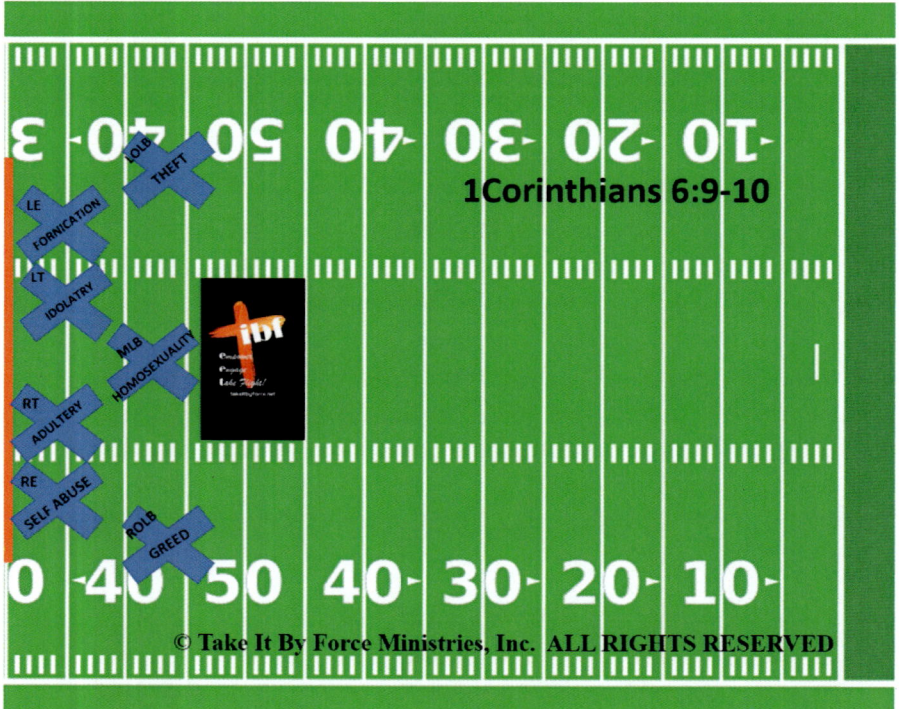

Graphic (13)

To round out the linebacker core in graphic (13) is the **(ROLB)- Right Outer Linebacker** of **greed**. Another term for this behavior is covet. When you covet what someone else has, you can lose focus of your own life. **Exodus 20:17** says, *"Thou shalt not covet thy neighbour's house, thou shalt not covet thy neighbour's wife, nor his manservant, nor his maidservant, nor his ox... nor any thing that is thy neighbour's."*

Time is the most important thing you have in life. Without it, you can do nothing. Don't spend it focusing on what others have. Be an original. Create your own pathway in life, using God's word as a blueprint. Minding your own business and focusing on your relationship with the Lord can be very fulfilling. **1Thessalonians 4:11** instructs us to, *"...study...do your own business, and..work with your own hands.."*

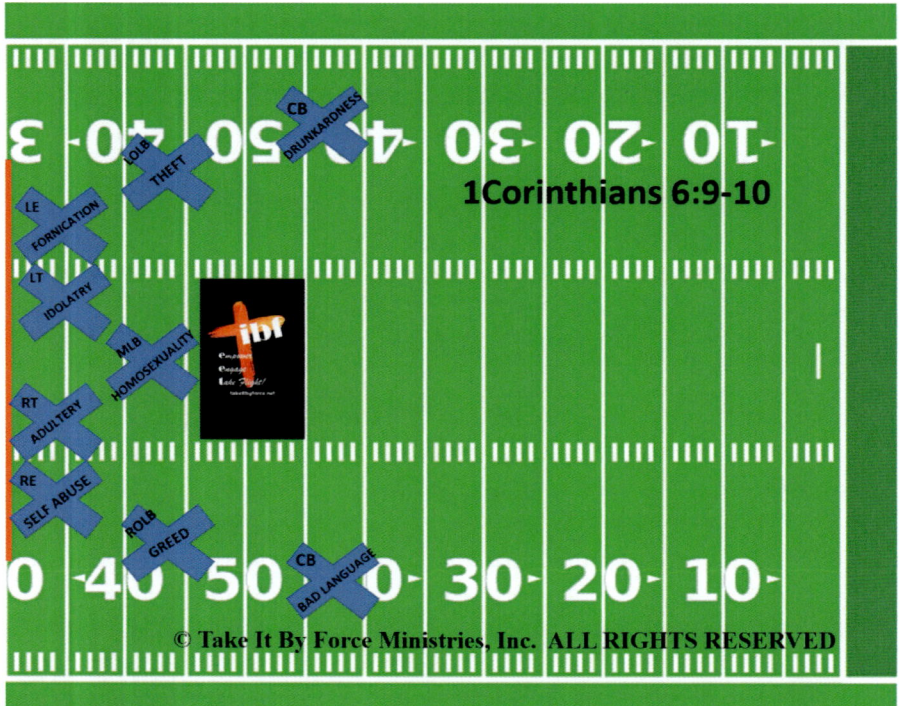

Graphic (14)

So far, we have looked at the defensive players who put pressure directly on the line of scrimmage. Now let's introduce those who cover the wide receivers. In graphic (14), these are known as the **(CBs)- Cornerbacks** of **drunkardness** and **bad language**. The CB is waiting to be in constant stride with the WR, to make it difficult to catch the ball, or intercept the pass.

Drunkardness can be defined as overconsumption. I think

overconsumption of social media is a challenge because it intercepts time that could be devoted towards more productive activity. The harmful exposure on social media, ranging from violent and sexual content, to bullying and harassment, is a danger zone.

Pick Up that Blitz! – Identify an area in your life where overconsumption is a blitz. Can you think of any opportunities that were missed? What can you do differently to withstand the blitz and utilize your time more wisely to advance your life forward?

_____

_____

_____

_____

_____

_____

_____

_____

_____

Bad language or reviling can be a turnoff. Build good character by keeping your written and verbal communication along with social media content clean. Employers, college admission offices, and scholarship committees can look at your social media platforms. It would be a shame to have an opportunity taken away because of filthy language and content. Keep in mind that you may need someone to write a letter of recommendation for you. Even when you're having a bad day, how and what you communicate says a lot about who you are and can determine if you get the recommendation. Stay away from verbally abusing others and strive to engage in conversations that will encourage and not belittle or provoke an individual to violence.

Now if the defense is unsuccessful at stopping the ball at the line of scrimmage or the corners, it must have a secondary plan in place. The secondary is the last opportunity to stop the ball from getting into field goal range or a touchdown. The last player Paul mentions in graphic (15) is the **(FS)- Free Safety** of **extortion**, which is scamming others just to get ahead.

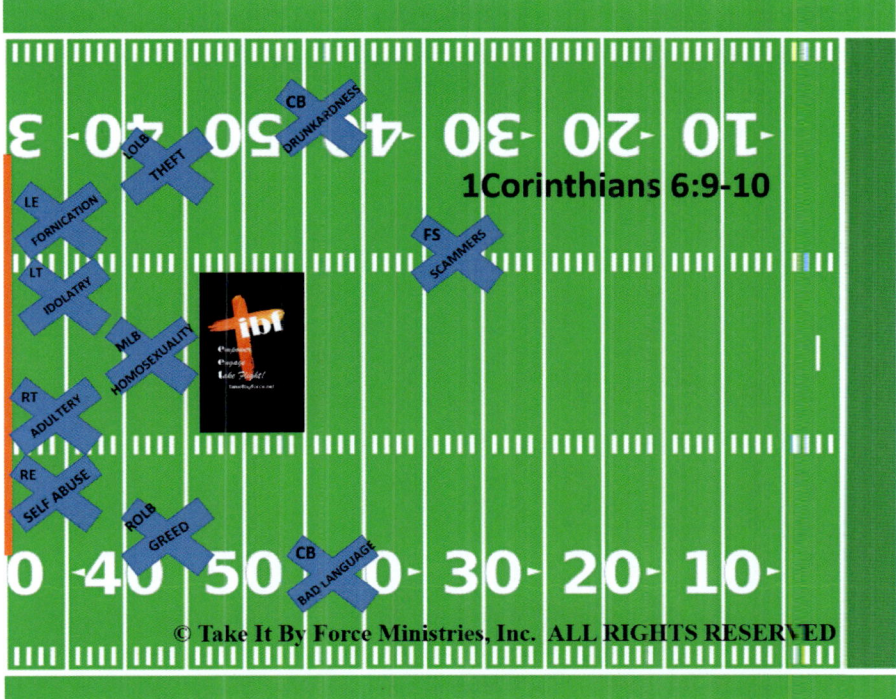

Graphic (15)

Never take advantage of people. It will get you nowhere fast. **Matthew 7:12** says, *"...whatsoever ye would that men should do to you, do ye even so to them..."* Treat others the way you want to be treated. That rounds out Paul's introduction of players on the devil's defense.

But there is one more in graphic (16).

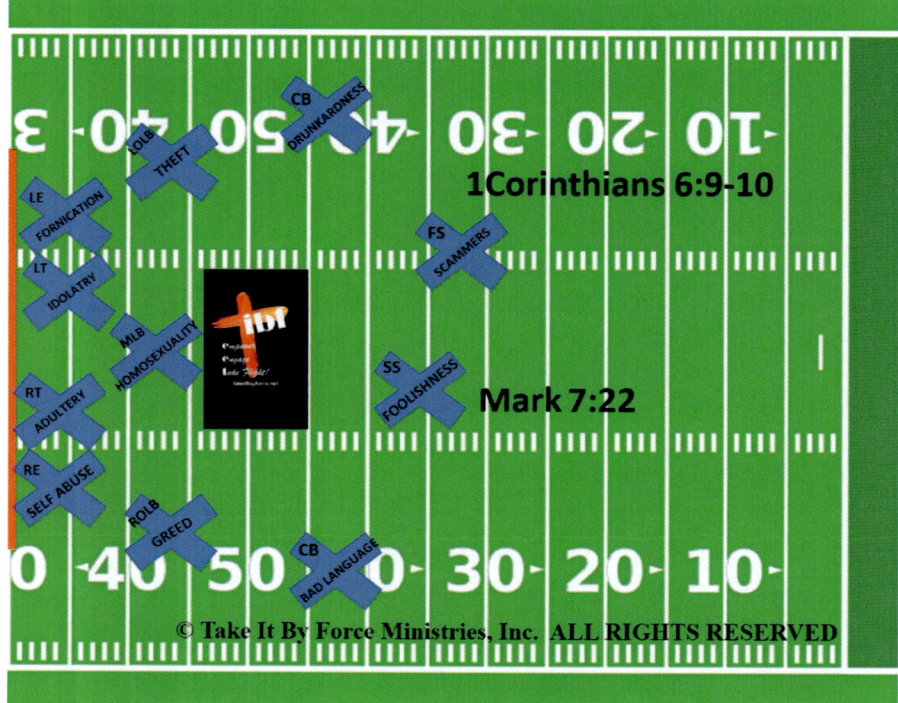

Graphic (16)

The final player is the **(SS)- Strong Safety** of **foolishness.**
The SS is a hybrid of its teammates. It covers the pass and
stops the run. Foolishness, just like the duties of a strong
safety, is a hybrid of its teammates on the devil's defense. It's a
blend of all unrighteousness.

To identify root causes that make a person unclean, Jesus
says in **Mark 7: 21-23**, *"...out of the heart...proceed evil
thoughts, adulteries, fornications, murders, thefts,*

*covetousness, wickedness, deceit, lasciviousness (lust), an evil eye, blasphemy, pride, **foolishness**: All these evil things come from within, and defile..."*

These things can take root in the heart through constant exposure. That's why it is important to know, from a biblical perspective, what is right and wrong in your environment, so you can make the decision not to model after wrong behavior. The devil's defense is real, and it has every intention of keeping you from living a victorious life in the Lord Jesus!

in the LORD JESUS!!

5- God's Offense

The offensive lineman tends to be the largest and strongest player on the field. Within a few quick steps, the lineman is to establish position, followed by a wrestling match with the defensive lineman. Thus, the offensive lineman absorbs a lot of contact while creating **opportunity** for the HB to advance down the field with the ball, during the running plays, and **time** for the QB to throw it on passing plays.

God understands that you need two things in life: opportunity and time to maximize it. That's why he sent his son Jesus Christ. While on his way to the cross, Jesus absorbed a lot of contact so that whosoever would believe in and have a relationship with him would not perish but have an opportunity at everlasting life. Dying on the cross was the greatest sacrifice given for mankind.

Being an offensive lineman can be a grievous task. It can be a position stricken with injury and afflicted with the pressure of a relentless defensive front! But, just as an offensive line puts its all into the game, for the advancement of the football, so did Christ become the ultimate offensive line in graphic (17) for the advancement of your life!

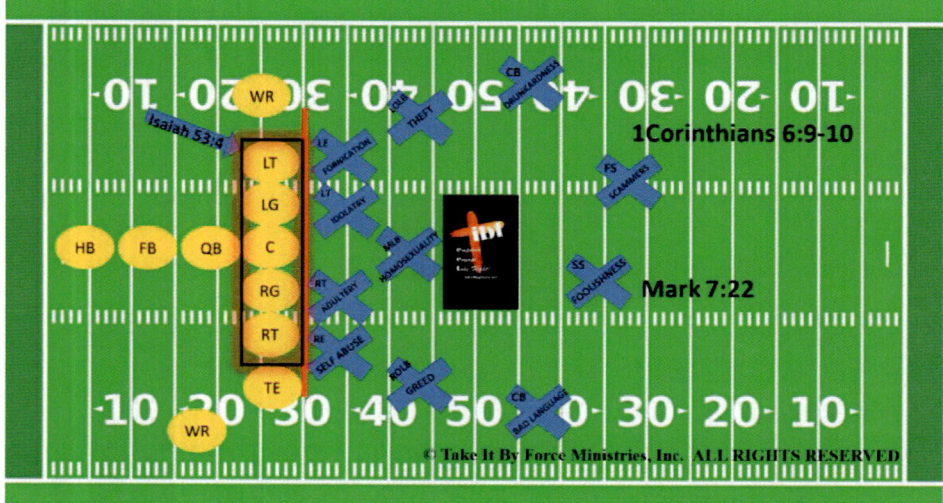

Graphic (17)

Isaiah 53:4 says, *"Surely he hath borne our griefs, and carried our sorrows...stricken, smitten..afflicted."* Christ absorbed your griefs and sorrows so that you do not get stuck by them when the devil's defense is blitzing you full force. I did not say that you will not encounter grief and sorrow for various reasons from time to time, but you must get up and press your way forward to the next down. He was afflicted so that you are not eliminated by the afflictions you sometimes face. Each day God wakes you up, it's a new opportunity to advance your life. Jesus Christ is your ultimate option for advancement beyond a life of guilt, shame, hurt, unforgiveness, depression, mental anguish and anxiety! Move the chains! FIRST DOWN in the Lord Jesus!

Time is valuable in the game, and the QB must be there mentally. God gets that. That's why Christ is his ultimate QB below in graphic (18).

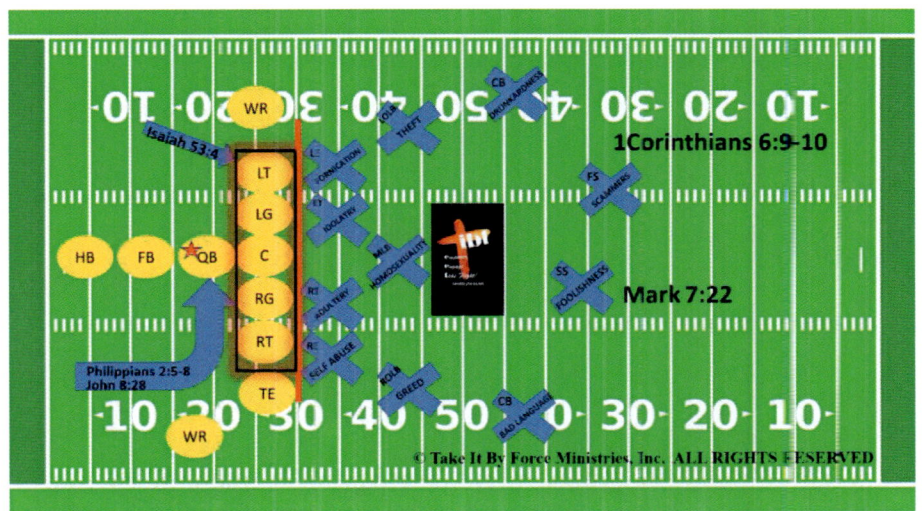

Graphic (18)

Philippians 2:5-8 says, *"Let this mind be in you, which was also in Christ Jesus: Who, being in the form of God, thought it not robbery to be equal with God: But made himself of no reputation, and took upon him the form of a servant, and was made in the likeness of men: And being found in fashion as a man, he humbled himself, and became obedient..."*

The **QB must know what to do** with the football. You must know what to do with your life. Start with the right mindset. Model after the mind of Christ, who did not try to make a name for himself but served the needs of others. Everything else just fell into place. He was humble and knew how to follow the playbook given to him by his father and his coach, God! Christ was teachable. Jesus said in **John 8:28**, *"...I do nothing of myself; but as my Father hath taught me, I speak these things."* You must be teachable and allow God's word to coach you. Over time, you learn how to make the right calls in your life.

The **QB speaks in the huddle**, that which is called in from the coach. That instruction gives the other players on the offense their purpose. So, if Christ is the ultimate QB, and he gives the word, then those who grab it and break from the huddle, should go to their respective positions ready to perform at an ultimate level too! Why? Because the Holy Ghost brings back to remembrance (just that fast), the instructions Christ just gave. Jesus said in **John 14:26**, *"...the Holy Ghost...shall teach you all things, and bring all things to your remembrance, whatsoever I have said unto you."* And as the play call resonates within them, the vibe of the ultimate quarterback becomes the vibe of the ultimate offense on the field! The QB is the face of the franchise. Christ is the image of the invisible God. Jesus said in **John 14:9**, *"...he that hath seen me hath seen the Father..."*

Now I have not physically seen Jesus, but I received him spiritually into my heart as Lord and Savior. And when I received him, I received his Father, the Holy Ghost, and their playbook, the Bible! Jesus said in **Matthew 10:40**, *"...he that receiveth me receiveth him that sent me."*

That's why it's good to accept Jesus as Lord and Savior, attend a good Bible teaching church on a regular basis, and receive some godly instruction for your life. So, when you return back to your respective place, you should feel empowered to move forward with your life! Move the chains! FIRST DOWN in the Lord Jesus!

On the Field! – Who or what is speaking into your life? What kind of godly instruction are you getting? Is your life moving forward in a godly direction? If it is not, what can you do differently?

_____

_____

_____

_____

_____

_____

_____

_____

The QB knows how to read the defense; that's called discernment. As I said earlier, learn how to read some of the circles you hang with. I did not say judge. I said discern. Have enough godly wisdom to say, "No thanks," and come up with a different play call for your life. Nothing is wrong with an audible! Nothing is wrong with serving the Lord! As a matter of fact, Jesus told the devil in **Luke 4:8**, "*...Get thee behind me, Satan: for it is written, Thou shalt worship the Lord thy God, and him only shalt thou serve.*"

On the Field! – Any defensive tendencies you want to put behind you, so you can have a clear path to the endzone in some areas of your life? What can you do to make that happen?

_____

_____

_____

_____

_____

_____

The QB knows how to scramble with the ball. A scramble occurs when there is a mad rush by the defense, and the pocket collapses. At that point, the QB must maneuver through the chaos to avoid a loss of yardage. Sometimes, you will find yourself standing alone in the pocket of truth, and there may be a mad rush to disassociate from you. That's okay, do what is righteous and move on to the next play with your life in hand. Jesus knew how to escape. After being truthful with a crowd of observers, they got angry with Jesus. **Luke 4:28-30** says, *"...they...rose up...that they might cast him down..But he passing through the midst of them went his way."* Learn how to pass on through and pass over.

The QB knows what direction the ball needs to take. Jesus said in **Mark 4:35,** *"Let us pass over unto the other side."* Jesus knew that the storm was ahead, but he knew his team needed a drill about faith. He also knew that on the other side of that play call was the opportunity to help someone in need. When you place your life into the hands of the Lord, he can direct you on a route that will develop your growth and release your potential to serve others.

 **On the Field!** – I can relate to that. When I was 15, the Lord led me to join a local church in my hometown. I was there for fourteen years. During that time span, I became a licensed minister, an ordained elder and youth pastor alongside my wife. From those years of experience, she and I were released to become founders and stewards of a local church, Dominion Tabernacle, Inc. and a non-profit, Take It By Force Ministries, Inc. For over twenty years, she and I, alongside our family of volunteers, have been able to serve the needs of many in the marketplace. Check out our website at **www.takeitbyforce.net**.

The QB knows his options and how to use them.
Maximizing the talent of the receivers and runners is essential to offensive success. Know what your options are in life and

maximize them. It's good to have a few things that you enjoy doing. For me, I enjoy preaching, teaching workshops, coaching recreation basketball, and interior designing.

Jesus knew what his options were. In **Luke 4:18-19** he said, *"The Spirit of the Lord is upon me, because he hath anointed me to preach the gospel to the poor; he hath sent me to heal the brokenhearted, to preach deliverance to the captives, and recovering of sight to the blind, to set at liberty them that are bruised, to preach the acceptable year of the Lord."* Jesus knew his options were to preach, heal, deliver, recover, and set free. He also knew that whatever he did, it had to be acceptable to his coach, God the Father. He said in **John 8:29**, *"And he that sent me is with me: the Father hath not left me alone; for I do always those things that please him."*

The coach doesn't leave the game. The coach has a presence on the sideline to help lead the team to victory! That's God's Offense. Psalm 24:1 says, "The earth is the Lord's, and the fulness thereof; the world, and they that dwell therein." God has everything at his disposal. His playbook is wide open. He can use whoever, whatever, whenever, however he wants to get the job done. When God's offense becomes your offense, the possibilities for your life are endless! Move those chains! FIRST DOWN in the Lord Jesus!

On the Field! – What are some things that you enjoy doing? How can God utilize your interests to help serve the needs of others?

_____

_____

_____

_____

_____

_____

_____

_____

_____

_____

in the LORD JESUS!!

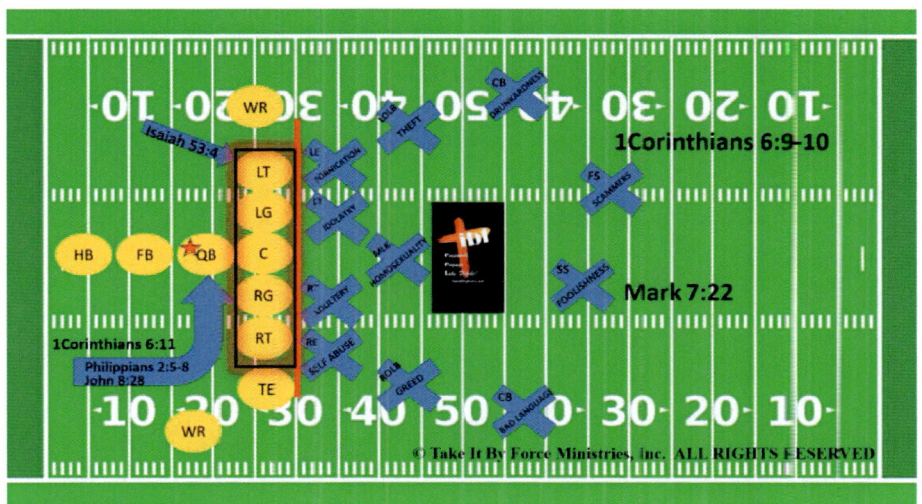

Graphic (19)

I n **1Corinthians 6:11**, The Apostle Paul acknowledges the defensive attack is real among his audience. He says, *"And such were some of you…"* Which means he understood there were some in the audience who struggled with the behaviors he mentioned.

As long as you live, there will be a fierce battle between the devil's defense and your offense. However, there is help available. Surrender your all to the Lord Jesus, and let him be your ultimate offense. When he takes command in graphic (19), your playbook opens up because you have a:

1.) strong offensive line & QB

2.) powerful receiving core

3.) dominant running game that can knock down a wall!

4.) sideline coach like none other, GOD!

And when you find yourself being knocked down by the defense, because it will happen; Paul says in verse **11**, *"...but ye are washed, but ye are sanctified, but ye are justified in the name of the Lord Jesus, and by the Spirit of our God."*

When Christ is your Lord and Savior, that means you are:

1.) ***washed****- cleaned up and ready for the next down*

2.) ***sanctified****-called to be on the team with Jesus*

3.) ***justified****- your relationship with Christ gives you the opportunity to stay on the team*

But do your part by going to practice and working out! (i.e., Church, Bible Study, Sunday School, Revival, Prayer). Have a heart to repent and live right regardless of how many times you may stumble and fall.

I hope this book has given you a different perspective on your life. It's a journey about strategy, struggle, being knocked down, getting back up and entering the endzone of VICTORY! Are you ready for some football? Let's GO!

If you don't know who Jesus is as Lord and Savior and would like to receive him, pray this prayer with a sincere heart, *"Dear Jesus, I am a sinner. But I believe that you died on the cross for my sins. I believe that you were buried, that God raised you from the dead, and you live now and forever more. Come into my heart; I receive you now as my Lord and Savior. Amen"*

If you are truly serious about your acceptance of the Lord Jesus and want to grow your relationship with him, please email us via our website: www.takeiybyforce.net. We would like to hear from you!

Leadership Training for Teens & Adults

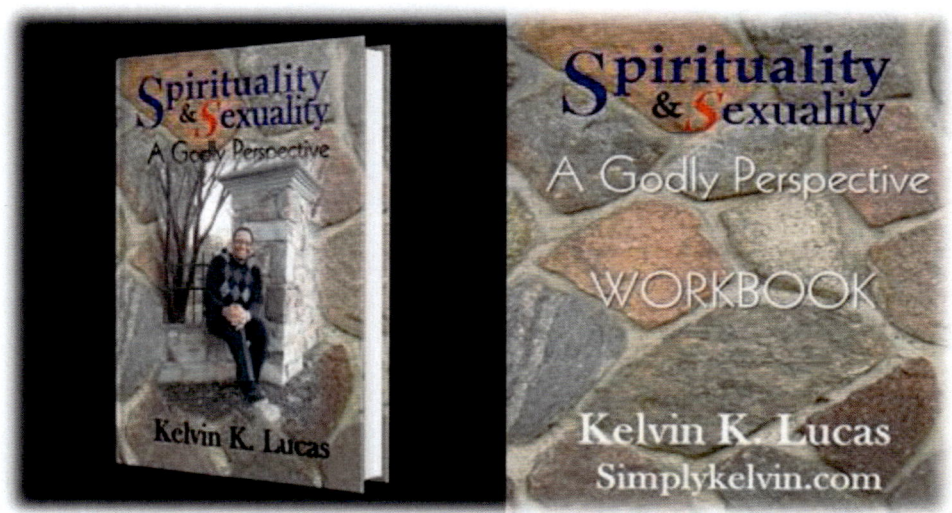

Personal Growth Workshop
for Teens & Young Adults

The Centers for Disease Control and Prevention suggest that young people aged 15–24 years acquire half of all new STDs in the U.S. and that one in four sexually-active adolescents has an STD, such as chlamydia or human papillomavirus (HPV). Compared with older adults, sexually-active adolescents aged 15–19 years and young adults aged 20–24 years are at higher risk of acquiring STDs.

Time is of the essence and God is challenging us regarding the importance of moral living. If you're a youth leader looking for a practical personal growth workshop for teens and young adults, reach out to us at Takeitbyforce.net!

Prolife Initiative

Since the 1973 Roe v. Wade Supreme Court decision, over fifty-four million babies have been aborted in centers around the nation. Of that number, more than 19 million of those babies were African American. Abortion is the number one killer in the African American community.

This initiative is designed to take a stand for the most vulnerable of all: the *unborn*. To learn more contact us at Takeitbyforce.net!

"And whoso shall receive one such little child in my name receiveth me." Matthew 18:5

ABOUT THE AUTHOR

Pastor Kelvin K. Lucas is a husband, father and leadership coach. He grew up in Rocky Mount, North Carolina. As a student attending Rocky Mount Senior High School, his journey towards servanthood began when he obtained his first job at the age of 16 at a local retail store. From that time, he began to embark upon learning a trade that has spanned over 25 years and has taught him the essential key to empowerment...SERVING.

After receiving a B.A. Degree in Business Management from N.C. State University, Pastor Lucas took his trade to the next level by accepting a corporate executive position with a major retailer. Through those years, he learned the leadership dimensions that would transition him into the next season of his life.

He was ordained as an Elder in July 1999, and in 2001 co-founded Take it By Force Ministries, a 501© (3) organization that offers community outreach events, leadership, creative writing, and life skills training for youth and young adults (www.takeitbyforce.net). He has authored three literary works, Spiritualty & Sexuality: A Godly Perspective, The Heart of an Entrepreneur: A Journey Through Time, and the TIME Leadership Academy Workbook.

Pastor Lucas truly understands the meaning of servanthood and has taken that passion to the community as a recreational sports coach, former PTA president, and mentor within the community at large.

He and his wife, Felicia, have been married since 1997. They have three wonderful children and are the Pastors of Dominion Tabernacle in Rocky Mount, North Carolina.

Notes

Notes

Notes

Contact Information

Website: www.simplykelvin.com

Facebook: Simply Kelvin Lucas

Instagram: Simplykelvinlucas

@Simplyklucas

simplykelvin.com

@simplykelvinlucas

His Glory Creations Publishing, LLC is an International Christian Book Publishing Company, established in 2017, which helps launch the creative works of new, aspiring, and seasoned authors across the globe, through stories that are inspirational, empowering, life changing or educational in nature, including fiction, non-fiction, memoirs, anthologies, poetry books, journals, children's books, and audio books.

DESIRE TO KNOW MORE?

CEO/Founder: Felicia C. Lucas

www.hisglorycreationspublishing.com

Email: hgcpublishingllc@gmail.com

Office Phone: 919-679-1706

Facebook: His Glory Creations Publishing

Instagram: His Glory Creations Publishing

YouTube: His Glory Creations Publishing